EARLY MORNING DREAMS FROM LATE NIGHT RISES

JACOBE MUNSELL
and BOBBI SUTHERLAND

Fulton Books
Meadville, PA

Published by Fulton Books 2024

ISBN 979-8-89427-337-2 (paperback)
ISBN 979-8-89427-338-9 (digital)

Printed in the United States of America

ACKNOWLEDGMENTS

Jacobe and Bobbi have been friends since 2015, when they both had the insane notion to try to join the navy and met at the recruiting office and then decided to quit that idea the next year at the same time. Since then, they have kept up on each other's adventures and life struggles, assisting where able. If friendship at a distance was ever considered perfect, they would be an example of just that.

Over these years, Jacobe would send Bobbi the poems and lyrics he wrote for her to review, which he never put forth any further. Bobbi decided to bring this to light and created a collection of his works with her photography mixed in. This created a work about phases of life and to bring light to the struggles life can bring someone, struggles that anyone can make it through with help from their friends.

Bobbi would like to thank the friends that stayed close through her travels across the United States. Even small conversations reminded her how much she is cared for in a world this big. She would also like to thank her late stepdad, Daryl Hazelwood, for pushing her to do what enjoys in life rather than working for just the money. Rest in peace.

Jacobe would like to thank his family, for without the trauma and trials, he would not have the life he has now.

Contents

NEW

BEGINNINGS

STARTING SOMETHING NEW IS SCARY AND ALMOST
UNREALISTIC. WE NEVER TRULY KNOW HOW
IT WILL GO. THE BIGGER IT IS, THE HARDER
IT FALLS; THE BIGGER IT IS, THE FASTER WE
RISE. CAN WE SAY WE AT LEAST TRIED?

**ALL GREAT BEGINNINGS START IN THE
DARK, WHEN THE MOON GREETS YOU
TO A NEW DAY AT MIDNIGHT.**

—**SHANNON L. ALDER**

CITY AND ME

Steam rises from underneath the sidewalks.
Stoplights change in a colorful cycle.
Sirens scream off in the distance.
It's the only place where you can be surrounded by
    small talks,
yet still feel alone in the world.
It's a complex coexistence,
that makes one feel spiteful.
The orange sunset turns skyscrapers into colossal
    bonfires.
Daytime hustle soon turns to nighttime peace.
Streetlights flicker as I walk past.
Everywhere I go feels like home,
when it's just the city and me.

Home in America

Music and sunburn at the races in Indiana,
Drum circle and wildlife in Florida,
Oktoberfest in the mountains of Georgia,
Fireworks and skipping rocks in North Carolina,
Having lunch with the Goddess of Love in Tennessee,
These places are home to me.
Experiencing the decades of Presley and Nirvana in
        Ohio,
Hotel birthday parties in Wisconsin,
Graduations in Minnesota,
Heartbreaks in Missouri,
These places are home to me.
Learning to sing and dance in Nebraska,
Chinese food with a harpist in Iowa,
Moonshine and Mennonites in Kentucky,
Hiking for art in California,
Loving the Heart of Dixie in Alabama,
These places are home to me.
Finding tattoo art in Illinois,
Seeing the sunrise in the mountains of Pennsylvania,

Falling asleep to the sound of the Turnpike in New
     Jersey,
Finding magic in New York,
These places are home to me.
There's a little bit of home,
Everywhere I go.
If home is where the heart is,
My heart is shattered.
The pieces are spread across America.

WHAT MADE HER BEAUTIFUL

When she flipped her hair,
and the clothes she would wear.
When she would make friends with strangers,
without the fear of danger.
When she got her heart broken,
and kept his gifts as a token.
This is what made her beautiful.

Taking Flight

For one moment, my soul takes flight.
As the ground disappears beneath my feet
Two wheels, open road
My heart racing the wind,
Without a care where it goes.
No fear as I give chase,
To sun and moon alike.
The thrill of the hunt
Shivering down my spine

Happy Beginnings

Freedom is what you do,
With what has been done to you.
Finishing one's goals,
Is finishing a life sentence.
Life can tear you down,
While death brings a happy ending.
Where is the happy beginning
That we so long for?

ONE LIFE

The bright light of a new beginning,
Crawling turns into walking,
Running to the playground grinning,
New school, new you, new friends,
Graduation becomes a challenge,
College an even bigger one to manage.
It all spins into a beautiful lie.
Eat, work, sleep, in the blink of an eye,
The painful truth becomes clear.
Death is a dark hood that is coming near.

DAYS
GONE BY

CRUNDEN MARTIN
MFG CO

A reminder of the past, to be content with the present, and to celebrate the future that beholds. Our pasts can hold us hostage to the darkest and coldest nightmares, blinding us to the warm light of what lies ahead. We must not forget to open our eyes to the realms of possibilities, stepping through the doors that open in front of us.

There is nothing like a dream to create the future.

—Victor Hugo

Invisible Man

When winter comes and a chill haunts the sun
I still feel aches in once broken bones
Where cracks run like cement riddled with weeds
And if I tell this to someone who has never
Fractured a rib or wrist
All I get in reply
Are accusations of lies

So when the ghost that haunts my life
Creeps through the vent beneath my bed
To weigh me down with chains of lead
It's no surprise at the answer
When I say I'm depressed

Because chronic illness is not visual
Until the black beneath the sunken eyes
Grows so bold

A black hole
Could open up and still look light
Compared to the sickness
You claim I fake yet only hide
In a mask of self-deceit

Wax and Wane

Take me
To the edge of your world
Where your soul rims the icy despair
Buried deep beneath your kind words

Take me
To the edge of your world
Where your heart lays in ashen black
Descended below your day warm smile

Take me
To all the places others fear
Where angels dare not tread
Hidden away from undaring eyes

Take me
And immerse me in your distant, bitter thoughts
Where I may learn to hold them
So I may also embrace your light

Gifts to the Sea

Upon the water, the flames dance
Ghosts of the days now gone
Shimmering among those blackened waves
Eagerly waiting gifts to hold
Beneath their lachrymose form
I give freely to them the memories
Earned beneath the glint of suns
Both relic and new are thrown
So that when morning breaks
I can face the empyrean chains
Binding soul to life

Weeping Willow

And suddenly like a wisp of autumn's breath,
We were strangers again
Nine years entwined in fate brought to rest
Beneath the boughs of a weeping willow
Where once, in my hands, you laid your head
Forever kept beneath those draping, verdant sallows
That now becomes a grave for eyes unmet

CYCLES

I never wanted this rage;
It was my inheritance,
From those who also inherited it.
The thorns pierce tired skin,
Holding tight to every moment
As I attempt to resist this fate
But I think this is all I am:
An unending fire in the dark;
A bloodied blade buried in the back;
A desperate kid screaming for help,
That never comes.

Pieces of Years

I wring my hands, a comfort motion
For a constant unrest I can't shake
In a body like a worn-out dishrag
My bones ache with the reality
All my words ran away with childhood dreams

I play along with the script
Pretending I don't wish for escape
As if a piece of myself isn't gone with every wind
Like the years that have passed me by
And I can't seem to follow behind

For one moment, I release the tension
My jaw unclamps its vise grip
Letting slip a breath held tight
Like a blade waiting to drop
And sever my grasp on this fight

Always You

I play your notes in long, somber timbres,
Next to the only empty wall on a crowded city street.
"How beautiful," I hear them say,
"If only he played something more cheerful."
But yours are the only strings I know.

I run my fingers across the strings,
And keys of others,
Feeling for the notes to click like yours.
But the attempt always ends in vain,
And I return to you at the end of the day.

I try to find solace in familiarity,
As my fingers ache to let you go.
But tighten again before the release.
Resting you once again at my knee,
And strumming the strings that bind me.

How Many Years

These lessons never seem to take their place
The knife digs deeper in my spine
And I smile through the pain
With blood behind my teeth
To keep your story straight

Sinking again into a mask
I'll be the bastard in your play
I'll hide my face from the light
If you promise to forget my name

Raking the edges of my heart
For any ounce of care
Fraying at the seams to hold on
And losing myself there
What does it take to make you see
The blame is yours to share

Sinking again into a mask
I'll be the bastard in your play
I'll hide my face from the light
If you promise to forget my name

I held on until my fingers ached
Sleepless and drowned by a drink
This storm is one I can't weather any longer
I'm done trying to be stronger

Take these words to your grave
With a nameless voice carrying them
Just a shadow in the background misplaced
Leave me out of sight, out of mind
I've got nothing left to say

Sinking again into a mask
I'll be the bastard in your play
I'll hide my face from the light
If you promise to forget my name

I held on until my fingers ached
Sleepless and drowned by a drink
This storm is one I can't weather any longer
I'm done trying to be stronger

Life and Death

I awoke from a dream today
It was one where everything changed
I was completely new
Yet everything still felt meaningless

I smoked a cigarette
Just to feel the pain
And I drank whiskey
Like it was water
Soon to disappear

My life—just another story
Maybe happier, but meaningless
All the same
I told the greatest thing to ever happen
To me that I loved her
And maybe she loved me too
But dreams fade and blur
Leaving behind a darker grey

I'm just another man
Not long for this world
These tired bones keep going

As they beg to quit
But I'll keep pushing
Until there's nothing left
It's just how I am

I smoked a cigarette
Just to feel the pain
And I drank whiskey
Like it was water
Soon to disappear

My life—just another story
Maybe happier, but meaningless
All the same
I told the greatest thing to ever happen
To me that I loved her
And maybe she loved me too
But dreams fade and blur
Leaving behind a deeper grey

Now this is where I am left
Another sleepless night
Staring at the pouring rain
One more cigarette, I tell myself
To make it feel alright
But not even whiskey numbs this pain

CALL OF THE VOID

THE VOID IS ALWAYS CALLING FOR US. FATE
WILL HAVE WHAT IT SEEKS. IT IS INEVITABLE,
THOUGH WE CAN POSTPONE AS LONG AS
FATE ALLOWS. WE JUST NEED TO KNOW
HOW TO MAKE THE MOST OF IT BEFORE
FATE RESIGNS OUR GREED FOR LIFE.

MAN'S FIRST EXPRESSION, LIKE HIS FIRST
DREAM, WAS AN AESTHETIC ONE. SPEECH
WAS A POETIC OUTCRY RATHER THAN A
DEMAND FOR COMMUNICATION. ORIGINAL
MAN, SHOUTING HIS CONSONANTS,
DID SO IN YELLS OF AWE AND ANGER
AT HIS TRAGIC STATE, AT HIS OWN
SELF-AWARENESS AND AT HIS OWN
HELPLESSNESS BEFORE THE VOID.

—BARNETT NEWMAN

ABOVE, BELOW

To reveal the solitude of the heavens
The curtain of grey clouds peeled back
In their dimmest hours
Alone, they ponder
Forlorn kings upon cold, mundane thrones
As above, the twilight shimmers
So below, the earth whispers
Broken breaths of life in the lonely void

Mortal Coil

There is a closure in death
The silencing of life
A last breath that closes
Curtains fall, the stain of crimson
In shadows of darkest desire
Immortality eats away hope

The ruins of unknown hope
Seals the mark of death
The snows of earnest desire
Chills the winds of life
And swords begin the spill of crimson
War becomes as day closes

Breath is the door that closes
When the heart arouses hope
In violent streaks of crimson
The seductive touch of death
To end all-warming life
Spelled by selfish desire

Fear of the raging desire
Envy blackens as night closes
Shaded gilts of scarring life
Illusions the mind into breaking hope
Until steeled by iron death
Poisoned by liquid crimson

Set fire to sweet crimson
Give into darkest desire
Ending the bleakest of life
Unchained as the scene closes
Time decays, shattering hope
Rusting the clockwork stoic life

Through bitter-biting life
Spiritual release flowers from sanctioned crimson
A cleansed touching to hope
Cobalt impurity marking the stained desire
Tears consume as steel closes
By means only understood through bladed death

Death is always intertwined with life
As the curtain closes, the color of crimson
Showing the faults of desire and hope

Absent Thoughts

When the last rose wilts
In its crystal grave
As the light pours in
I'll close the blinds

When the last word is spoke
In a quiet voice
As the door swings shut
I'll turn out the lights

When the last ember cools
In the hearth unkept
As the flame snuffs out
I'll yield to the night

When the last chore is done
In this silent home
As the shower runs cold
I'll end my life

Memorial Nights

Your silent friction thunders in my eyes
Calling me to the darkened sky
The waxen light falters for a moment
As your violet veins split the night
With the fury of seraphic might
The primordial rage stirs within
Calling the days gone
A reminder of all that was and will be
Spanning infinity in your eyes

Grave Chills

Here lies the sleeping hollow
Lying deep inside the grave.
The chains digging into my wrists
I am nothing here but a slave.
The embers dying now,
Not a heart beats in this cell.
Bleeding quietly, patiently waiting for steel lips
Such a darkly beautiful kiss.
To feel the lights, fade away
I would erase the scars,
If only to see the stars.

Turn back to the pages of life,
Reduced to a simple nothingness.
In the cold, twelve rings out,
From the pendulums midnight approaches.
Death invades into my chest,
Though I do not fear for the future.
No other choice presents itself,
But to follow and welcome fate.

Misery as a lonely companion,
And emotion devoid of all but hatred.
The darkest days have come.
Fall away now, be ready to hurt.
Nothing left to do, just burn.
Just burn away into ash,
For it is a weapon which condemns.
Only to find a salvation.
As ends meet, show through
The stained light to the next
Grave to haunt us in the cold.

My Soul to Keep

Beautiful in every way
Roses once lovely now wilted
I look alive to the naked eye
Inside I'm far beyond the grave
I've begun my yearning for death
The chorus is all I beg

Ashes to ashes
Dust to dust

For cerement's cold embrace, I lust
A dream wrapped in miasmal whispers
Bleeding the fog from my wrists
Right through the cracks I have fallen
White wings turned to blackened bone

Welcome to hell
Welcome home

My demons whisper when I lay me down to sleep
And never find worth in the words
My soul to keep

CALL OF THE VOID

Your shadowed light ever my guide
As I make my way to nowhere exact
Driven by my soul supine
Shrouded by the brace of Nyx
Hands on the wheel relaxed
My heart remains remiss
Hanging by a thread endless
Our faces meet for the last
Dear moon, I'll miss your caress

STOP

About the Authors

Bobbi Sutherland is twenty-six years old and was born in Sarasota, Florida. She moved a lot growing up and has lived in six different states so far, her favorite being western Montana. She wrote short stories and poetry throughout grade school but really enjoyed writing research papers during her undergraduate years at the University of South Florida. She currently holds a BA in psychology and welding certifications. Her next goal is to complete a master's in forensic psychology. Her hobbies include traveling, hiking, and photography.

Jacobe Munsell is twenty-seven years old and was born in Flint, Michigan, though he currently resides in Lafayette, Indiana. He started writing poems and song lyrics when he was ten years old and loves art in all its forms. His hobbies include riding motorcycles and practicing historical European martial arts. He also enjoys Magic: the Gathering and Dungeons and Dragons.